Team Up! 4

Suzanne Roy
Kathleen Vatcher

Cooperative-Learning Consultant
Jim Howden

ERPI ÉDITIONS DU RENOUVEAU PÉDAGOGIQUE INC.

5757, RUE CYPIHOT, MONTRÉAL (QUÉBEC) H4S 1R3
TÉLÉPHONE : (514) 334-2690 • TÉLÉCOPIEUR : (514) 334-4720
erpidlm@odyssee.net

ENGLISH AS A SECOND LANGUAGE – GRADE 4

Project editor: **Jeanine Floyd**

Cover and book design, page layout: **Dumont Gratton**

Photo researcher: **Michel Malouin**

Illustrations:
Christine Battuz: pp., 23, 27, 50, 54, 60, 73, 81, 101, 102, 103, 104 105, 106, 107, 109, 112, 119, 160, 167, 170, 178, 183, 190, 191

Daniel Dumont: pp. 1, 4, 6, 9, 19, 22, 25, 28, 40, 44, 45, 46, 47, 49, 51, 64, 65, 67, 78, 89, 96, 98, 106, 118, 127, 137, 140, 141, 143, 144, 146, 155, 165

Jean-Paul Eid: pp. 2, 6, 11, 12, 14, 15, 16, 17, 18, 19, 20, 21, 29, 37, 41, 55, 59, 60, 62, 63, 81, 82, 84, 89, 90, 100, 108, 112, 116, 117, 119, 120, 121, 124, 125, 128, 131, 132, 133, 134, 135, 136, 138, 140, 149, 150, 156, 157, 158, 166, 168, 172, 179, 181, 187

Lucie Faniel: pp. 7, 13, 24, 32, 33, 34, 35, 36, 48, 52, 55, 56, 60, 65, 69, 72, 73, 86, 91, 97, 116, 122, 126, 130, 139, 142, 143 145, 146, 164, 169, 170, 173, 178, 182, 186

Marie-Claude Favreau: pp. 4, 10, 28, 30, 34, 38, 42, 46, 51, 57, 60, 61, 68, 78, 79, 87, 91, 99, 111, 114, 115, 129, 151, 155, 163, 165, 170, 174, 175, 180, 184, 185, 192, 193, 194

Caroline Mérola: pp. 5, 20 31, 53, 58, 60, 64, 80, 94, 95, 96, 98, 118, 148, 154, 171, 188, 189

Ninon Pelletier: pp. 39, 70

Photographs:
Denis Gendron: pp. 3, 9, 21, 31, 41, 51, 60, 69, 81, 88, 91, 93, 100, 112, 122, 123, 130, 140, 152, 161, 171

Johnnie Eisen: p. 43

Megapress: p. 8, 66, 83, 92, 147

Réflexion: pp. 66, 83, 92, 113, 147

The story *Jenny Lives on Hunter Street* is reproduced by permission of Nelson Price Milburn Limited, New Zealand.
© 1992 Text by Ngaire Ravenswood
© 1992 Illustrations by Geoff Kelly
© 1992 Nelson Price Milburn Limited
Distributed in Canada as part of THE BOOK BANK COLLECTION by Scholastic Canada

Cirque du Soleil
Alegria, Mystère, Nouvelle Expérience and *Saltimbanco* posters pp. 156, 161, illustrator: Michel Thomas Poulin
Quidam poster pp. 155, 156, illustrator: François Chartier; photographer: Ron Levine
Nouvelle Expérience pp. 153, 157, 159, 161: Anne Lepage (trapeze), photographer: Al Seib; Jinny Jacinto, Nadine Binette, Laurence Racine, Isabelle Chassé (contortionists), photographer: Jean-François Leblanc; David Lebel, Stacey Bilodeau, Bruce Bilodeau, André St-Jean, Frank Michel, Gilles Lacombe, Philippe Chartrand, Faon Bélanger (Korean plank), photographer: Jean-François Leblanc; Vasily Demenchoukov (chair-balancing), photographer: Al Seib, David Lebel, Cécile Ardail (clowns), photographer: Al Seib; France Labonté (Madame Corporation), photographer: Al Seib

Franco Dragone, producer, p. 159, photographer: Al Seib,
Guy Laliberté, founding president, p. 159, photographer: Ronald Maisonneuve

Acknowledgments

We wish to acknowledge the help of the following people in the publication of *Team Up! 4*:

Brenda Bossé, École Sainte-Lucie, C.S. Val d'Or; Robert Gauvin, Collège Saint-Jean-Bosco, C.S. Memphrémagog; Daniel Guay, École Adrien-Guillaume, C.S. Seigneurie; Guy Lapalme, École Point-du-Jour, C.S. Le Gardeur; Clélia Tulini, École Victor-Thérien, C.S. Sault-Saint-Louis, the members of the Reading Committee: Johanne Denhez, Robert Ridyard and Julie Sheper; Tamara Silver, Thomas Nelson Australia; Emmanuella St-Denis, Cirque du Soleil; Georges Laoun Opticien (glasses); and our models, Léa Beaudin, Félix Malo and Lola Wilhelmy.

To my mother, Edwina (S. R.)

Dépôt légal : 1er trimestre 1998
Bibliothèque nationale du Québec
Bibliothèque nationale du Canada
Imprimé au Canada

ISBN 2-7613-0830-1

1234567890 ML 987
2715 ABCD JS12

Contents

À toi qui commences à apprendre l'anglais!

Savais-tu qu'il est très utile de parler plus d'une langue?

Imagine le plaisir que tu pourrais avoir à suivre une émission de télévision en anglais ou à te faire des amis anglophones!

Alors dépêche-toi d'ouvrir ton manuel *Team Up! 4*. Il contient un grand nombre d'activités aussi amusantes qu'intéressantes: des jeux, des histoires, des dialogues, des petits projets et bien d'autres surprises encore. Tu verras, ce peut être très agréable d'apprendre une deuxième langue.

Toutes ces activités te permettront de vivre des expériences emballantes: échanges avec des jeunes de ton âge, voyages dans d'autres pays, séjours dans des familles étrangères, etc. Et tout se déroule en anglais! N'est-ce pas excitant!

Pour te guider dans ces nombreuses expériences, *Team Up! 4* te propose différents moyens que tu pourras utiliser seul(e) ou en équipe.

Ouvre bien grands tes yeux et tes oreilles et n'hésite pas à te joindre à notre groupe.

Les auteures

All about Us

Playing tennis   **Dancing**   **Listening** to music   **Playing** the flute   **Watching** TV

Meeting people

To introduce yourself to someone, or introduce someone to another person, or to say hello or goodbye (5.1)

It's very important to get to know each other. Find out how to do it.

▶ Read the expressions.

▶ Use them to introduce two classmates to each other.

William, meet Susan. Susan, this is William.

Nice to meet you, Susan.

Hi, William. Pleased to meet you.

Hooray, for the class!

To say who you are (1.1)

> Who are you? Let's make a team!
> ▶ Listen to your classmates.
> ▶ Give your name and birthdate.

HELP WINDOW

Personal identification

What is your name?
My name is Suzie.

How old are you?
I'm nine.

When is your birthday?
My birthday is on September 12.

What grade are you in?
I'm in grade four.

Where do you live?
I live in Montreal.

What is your address?
235 Fisher Street

What is your telephone number?
555-4628

HOORAY!

Same or different?

To understand what someone likes, dislikes, wants or prefers (1.2)

What do you like to do in your spare time?

▶ Listen to some students talk about their pastimes.

▶ Find your favourite pastime.

ACTIVITY 4

Fact or fiction?

To describe yourself and other people
(1.4)

> All about me.
> ➤ Think of three facts about yourself.
> ➤ Change one fact into fiction.
> ➤ Tell your classmates.

FACTS TO TELL YOUR FRIENDS

if you are tall or short

how tall you are

if your hair is long or short

the colour of your eyes

the colour of your hair

Name _____
Date of birth _____
Address _____
_____
Telephone number _____
Age ____ Grade ____
Hair colour _____
Eye colour _____
Height _____

HELP WINDOW

To describe yourself, you can say:

I'm tall.
My eyes are brown.
My hair is black.

I'm short.
My hair is short.

I'm 120 centimetres.
My eyes are hazel.
My hair is blond.
My hair is long.

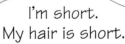

Who are we?

To understand someone's description of himself or herself (1.4)

Let's learn about each other.

▶ Read the information on your card.

▶ Ask your classmates the questions.

The inside-outside circle game

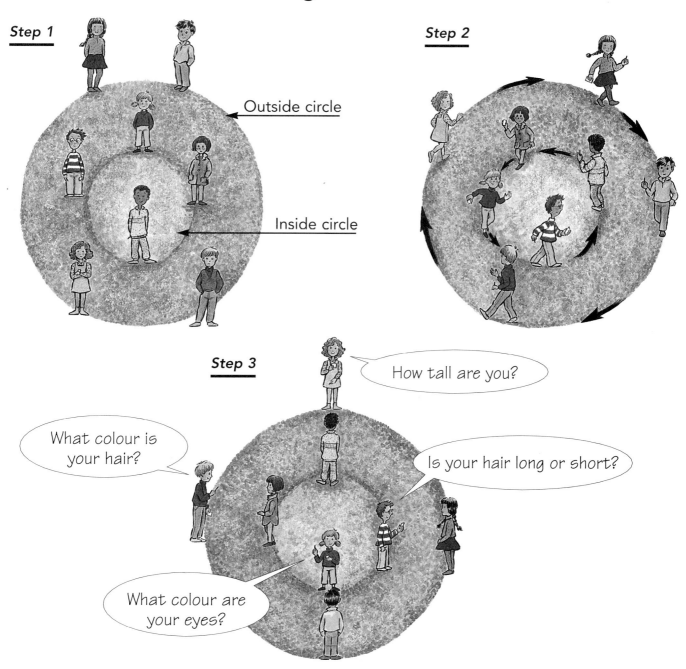

Step 1

Outside circle

Inside circle

Step 2

Step 3

How tall are you?

What colour is your hair?

Is your hair long or short?

What colour are your eyes?

7

CLOSURE

You will understand and give information about your personal experiences and the experiences of people close to you. (1.0)

Let's find out who's who.

► Look at the game card.
► Use the five ID cards and make your own game card.
► Find the right classmates.

	LIVES in Montreal	BIRTHDAY January 15	HAIR COLOUR blond	EYE COLOUR brown
AGE 9 years old		AGE 10	HAIR short	LIVES in Brossard
ADDRESS 124 du Coulis, Napierville	BIRTHDAY in September		HEIGHT tall	LIVES in Sherbrooke
BIRTHDAY June 27	HEIGHT 150 cm	BIRTHDAY April 15		HEIGHT 120 cm
HAIR COLOUR black	EYE COLOUR blue	HAIR long	BIRTHDAY in September	

Check-up TIME

This is what I learned.

1

I can greet someone.

I can introduce my friend.

2

I can give my name.

I can talk about myself.

I can give my telephone number.

I can say what grade I'm in.

I can give my address.

I can give my birthday.

I can say what I like to do.

I can give my age.

3

I can say what colour my eyes are.

I can say if I'm short or tall.

I can say what colour my hair is.

I worked well.

I moved quietly.

All about me

Absent-minded Alex

Are you forgetful?

To understand someone's description of himself or herself (1.4)

Do you forget things? Let's find out.

▶ Listen to the questions.

▶ Answer Yes or No.

13

ACTIVITY 2

The story, part one

To understand the major elements of a story: characters, conflict, events (3.1)

Absent-minded Alex has a problem. Can you guess what it is?

▶ Listen to the story.
▶ Find out about Alex.

At home

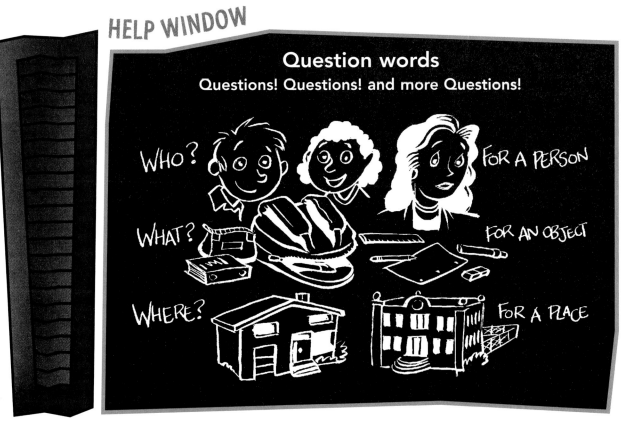

HELP WINDOW

Question words
Questions! Questions! and more Questions!

WHO? — FOR A PERSON

WHAT? — FOR AN OBJECT

WHERE? — FOR A PLACE

Where are my things?

To understand what a person or thing is
(2.1)

Poor Alex! He forgot his school supplies.

► Read what is on Alex's mind.

Oh! I forgot my eraser at school. I forgot my book! Where is my notebook? Where is my ruler? Where are my colouring pencils? I'm so forgetful!

ALEX

The story, part two

To understand a description of the major elements of a story: characters, conflict, events (3.2)

There are good days and there are bad days. Is Alex having a good day or a bad day?

▶ Listen to what happens to Alex next.

▶ Then look at the scenes at the bottom of page 18.

▶ Decide if the situation is a happy or a sad one for Alex.

Happy or sad?

The story, the conclusion

To say whether you like a story and what you feel about it (3.4)

Everyone can change if they want to. Let's see how Alex changes.

▸ Listen to the conclusion of the story.

▸ Say how you feel about the story.

HELP WINDOW

Reacting to a story

I think it's interesting.

Boring!

Great story!

Super!

Cute!

It's O.K.

I didn't really like it!

Right on!

The complete story

You will understand a story and react to it. (3.0)

Can you remember the story?
▶ Describe the missing events.

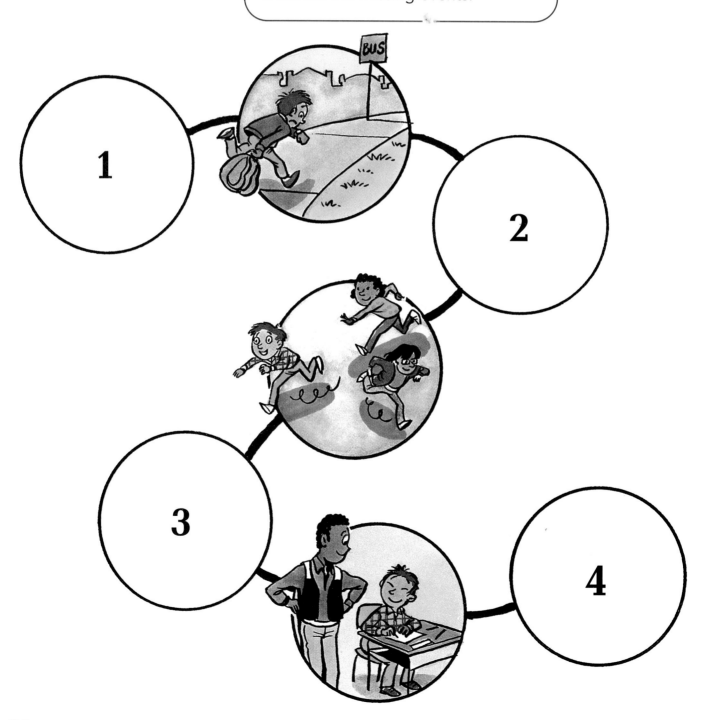

check-up TIME

This is what I learned.

1 I can name my school supplies.

2 I can name the characters from the story.

3 Who is forgetful?
What did Alex forget?
Where did Alex forget his schoolbag?

4 I think "Absent-minded Alex" was great.
I think "Absent-minded Alex" was fun.

I moved quietly in my group.

I took turns.

I worked quietly.

21

Absent-minded Liz?

Happy Birthday!

Birthday celebrations

To understand what a person or thing is
(2.1)

Let's find out about birthday celebrations.

► Listen to the text.
► Then complete the puzzle.

1 We eat ■■■■■ and candies at parties.

2 Funny people: ■■■■■■■

3 Origin of birthday parties: ■■■■■■■■■

4 Two ■■■■■■■■■ sisters composed a birthday song.

5 An old celebration was called ■■■■■■■■■■■.

25

Birthdays around the world

People celebrate their birthdays differently around the world. Let's find out what they do.

▶ Listen to how different people celebrate their birthdays.

▶ Find the illustration of each celebration.

Birthday calendar

To say who you are (1.1)

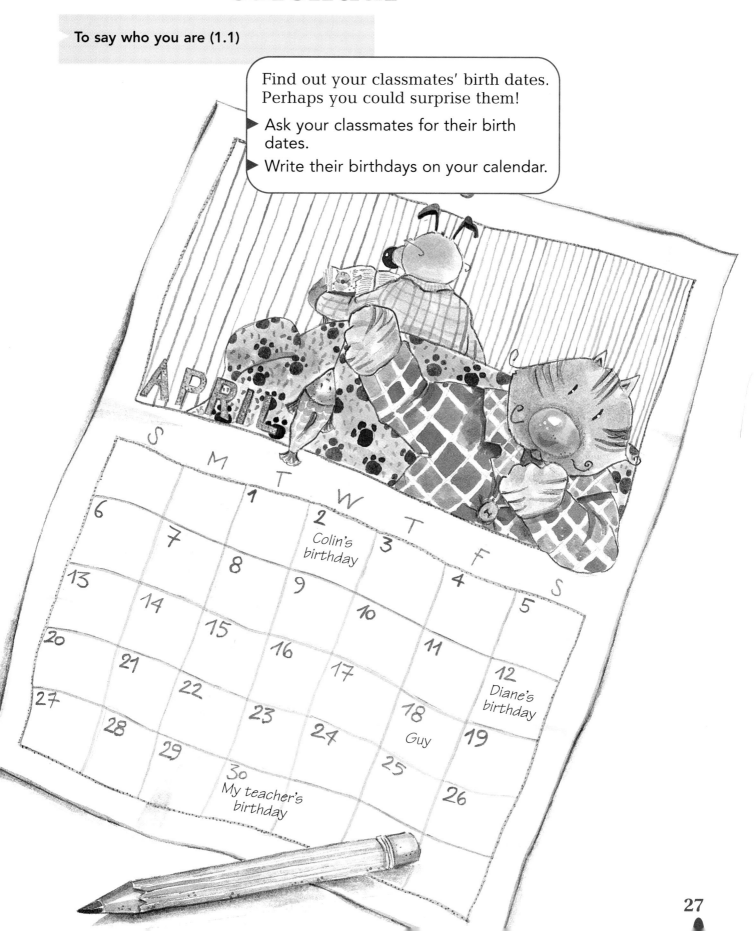

Find out your classmates' birth dates. Perhaps you could surprise them!

► Ask your classmates for their birth dates.

► Write their birthdays on your calendar.

Let's have a suggestion box.

To ask someone to do something or to go somewhere (4.6)

We can celebrate special occasions in many ways. Suggest something special to do on your classmates' birthdays.

▶ Think of something special.
▶ Write it on a piece of paper.
▶ Put it in the suggestion box.

HELP WINDOW

How to make a suggestion

Say:

Let's go to my house.
Let's play a game.
Let's listen to music.

We could go to my house.
We could play a game.
We could listen to music.

How about a movie?
How about a game?
How about some music?

Planning something special

To understand instructions (4.1)

To ask someone to give you information or to explain something (5.3)

Celebrations are fun, if they are well planned.

➤ Read the guide and find out what to do.

➤ Ask your teacher for help if necessary.

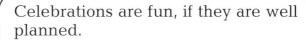

PLANNING GUIDE

What?	**Make** the suggestion.
How?	**Get** the instructions from your teacher. **Read** them to the group.
What material?	**Write** a list of the materials you need. **Ask** your teacher for the materials or **bring** them from home.
Who?	**Decide** who cuts, writes, colours and reads.

You will understand and give information about things outside your everyday life. (2.0)

You will understand and give information about activities related primarily to school life. (4.0)

Now prepare your celebration.

▶ Remember: Work quietly.
Keep on track.
Tidy up before you leave.

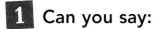 **Check-up** **TIME**

This is what I learned.

1 **Can you say:**

Who wrote the Happy Birthday song?

Where birthday parties began?

How Japanese people celebrate birthdays?

How you celebrate your birthday?

How children celebrate birthdays in the Netherlands?

2 **Can you** suggest ideas?
Can you follow instructions?

Did you work well in your group?

Did you listen to your teammates' ideas?

Did you share ideas?

How to make a pineta

YOU WILL NEED

- 2 biodegradable garden pots *or* 1 inflated balloon covered with glued newspaper strips
- glue
- cardboard paper, tissue paper, birthday wrapping paper, aluminum foil
- yarn, string, coloured ribbons
- poster paint (gouache)
- candy and/or party favours

INSTRUCTIONS

☞ Glue the 2 pots together or prepare the balloon.

☞ Tie the string around the pot securely and leave a long end to hang the pineta.

☞ Add cones, cylinders and squares to give it a shape and features (ears, legs, tail, etc).

☞ Use different coloured paper and paint to decorate it.

Different Families

Meet Amélie's family

To understand an introduction to another person or when a person says hello or goodbye (5.1)

Meet my family. They're great!

► Listen to Amélie talk about her family.
► Work out who's who.

Me, 1989

Josée, 1996

Eric, 1992

Mom's birthday

Me and Dad

Our house

My family

Reuben's family

To understand how someone feels and
what someone is going to do (1.5)

Reuben's family is different from
Amélie's. But he also has special
feelings for his family.

▶ Listen to Reuben talk about his family.
▶ Decide how he feels.

HELP WINDOW

Words to express feelings

Reuben is **happy**.
Reuben is **glad**.
Reuben is **not sad**.
Reuben **feels good**.

Reuben is **sad**.
Reuben is **not happy**.
Reuben is **unhappy**.
Reuben **feels upset**.

Lee's family

To understand comparisons between the world of a story, and yourself and your own experiences (3.3)

Lee's family is different from Amélie's and Reuben's families. Find out more about them.

▸ Listen to Lee describe her family.
▸ Compare her family with Reuben's family.

Jason's family

To understand the major elements of a story: characters, conflict, events (3.1)

Jason tells us about his family. Let's find out about them.

▶ Read Jason's story.
▶ Complete the family map.

My Family, by Jason Trehan

In my family there's my mom, my dad, my brother and my sister. Oh! I almost forgot, and Charlie, my dog.

Last year, my parents separated. From Monday to Friday, Charlie and I live with my mother. My brother and sister live with my dad. On weekends, my brother and sister, Charlie and I all live together with one of our parents.

I felt sad when my parents separated. But now I'm O.K. My parents explained that they love us all very much. And we love them too!

My family

To understand who someone is (1.1)

To introduce yourself (5.1)

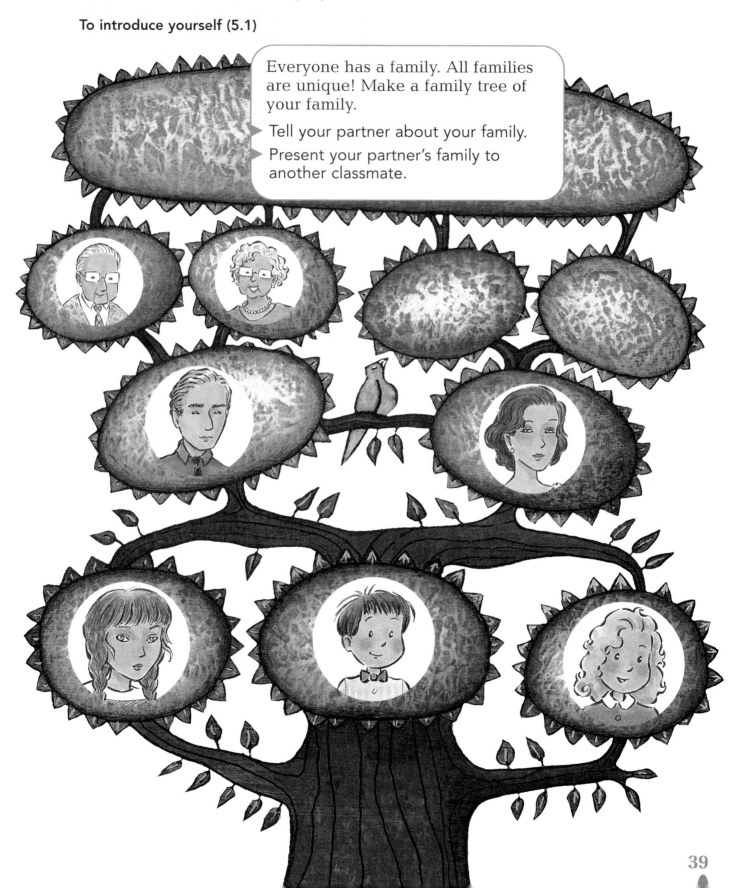

Everyone has a family. All families are unique! Make a family tree of your family.

Tell your partner about your family.

Present your partner's family to another classmate.

CLOSURE

You will understand and give information about your personal experiences and the experiences of people close to you. (1.0)

You will understand a story and react to it. (3.0)

Tell us about your family.
▶ Bring something special that belongs to someone in your family.
▶ Tell your partner about the object and the person who owns it.

This is my grandmother's paintbrush. She paints beautiful pictures for me. I think grandmothers are special. I visit my grandmother every week.

Check-up TIME

This is what I learned.

How many people are there in your family? Can you introduce them to a friend?

Can you compare your family with your friend's family?

How many people are there in your friend's family? Can you name them?

Did you celebrate differences?

Did you help your partner?

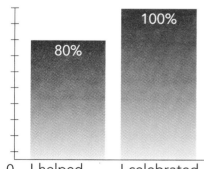

100%

80%

0   I helped   I celebrated
     my partner.   differences.

Tighten your family bonds

1. Say a kind word to everyone in your family before you go to school.

You're the best dad!

2. Participate in family reunions and parties.

3. Write a letter or send an audio-tape to your grandparents.

4. Start a family round-robin letter. Family 1 starts the letter and sends it to family 2. Family 2 adds to the letter and sends the whole letter to family 3, and so on.

5. Write thank-you notes to family members who have done something special for you.

6. Send cards to family members who have done something special for you.

7. Draw something special for someone in your family.

8. Watch a special TV program together.

9. Send your school picture to your cousins, aunts and uncles. And don't forget your grandparents!

10. Use e-mail to write to family members who live far away.

Tender, Loving Care

fish

dog

take for a walk

rabbit

bird

change the cat's litter

hamster

pet the cat

cat

horse

playing with a ball

chewing on a shoe

hiding under the rug

drinking from the aquarium

perching on the lamp

eating the plant

Animal talk

To understand what you must do (4.4)

Pets tell you what they need. What must you do?

▶ Look at the illustrations.
▶ Listen to what the pet owners say.
▶ Write down what you must do.

1

Change the litter.

4

Feed it.

2

Play with it.

Pet it.

3

Give it water.

5

HELP WINDOW

Use **must** and **have to** for obligation

You must listen!

You have to eat!

Take it for a walk.

6

A quiet moment

To understand what someone likes, dislikes, wants or prefers (1.2)

That night

Talking to your pet makes you feel better. Your pets know if you like them or not.

▶ Listen to the story.
▶ Decide if Matthew likes his pets or not.

I hope my mother will change her mind.

Does Matthew like his pets?

HELP WINDOW

LIKE	DON'T LIKE
I **like** dogs. Dogs are my favourite animals.	I **don't** like cats. Cats are not my favourite pets.
You **like** dogs. *He* **likes** dogs. *She* **likes** dogs.	*You* **don't like** cats. *He* **doesn't like** cats. *She* **doesn't like** cats.

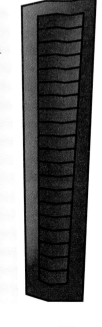

Pet care

To give instructions (4.1)

> If you have a pet, you must take care of it. Do you know what to do?
>
> ► Look at the chart on pet care.
> ► Make a chart for your own pet.

	Horse	Guinea pig	Rabbit
HOUSE	• Barn or stable for shelter • Pasture	• A cage — use aquarium but not a bird cage	• A cage for indoors and a sheltered cage outdoors
FOOD	• Buy hay and grain. • Feed it twice a day. • Give it water.	• Buy pellets. • Give it water.	• Buy pellets. • Give grass and hay. • Feed once a day.
CARE	• Feed, groom and exercise it once a day.	• Clean cage once a week.	• Clean cage once a week. • Groom it every day.
ATTENTION	• Needs a lot of attention • Ride it often.	• Needs little attention	• Needs a lot of attention • Hold it often.

The promise

To understand the major elements of a
story : characters, conflict, events (3.1)

The next morning

> Will Matthew have to give up his
> pets? Let's find out.
> ▶ Listen to the conclusion of the story.
> ▶ Illustrate what happens.

> But Mom, I love them!

You will understand and give information about activities related primarily to school life. (4.0)

What is your favourite pet? Tell us about it.

▶ Choose a pet you like.
▶ Make a poster for Animal Kindness Week.

Check-up TIME

This is what I learned.

Can you name the characters in the story?

What must you do with your dog?

Let it go outside.

Play with it.

Feed it or give it water.

What is your favourite pet?

I like horses.

What animal don't you like?

I don't like cats!

I encouraged others. I worked well.

I participated in my team.

I feel good about my work.

Animal read-a-thon!

Magic Time!

What do you know?
What do you know?

To describe a personal experience (1.6)

> Have you ever seen a magic show?
> Tell us about it.
>
> ▶ Think about what you saw and heard.
> ▶ Tell your partner about the show.

Abracadabra

Hocus-pocus

Make a magic wand

To understand instructions (4.1)

To understand someone who asks for help (4.2)

> Do you have a magic wand? Here's
> how to make one.
>
> ▶ Read the instructions.
> ▶ Make your magic wand.

Material

1 Place all your material on your desk.

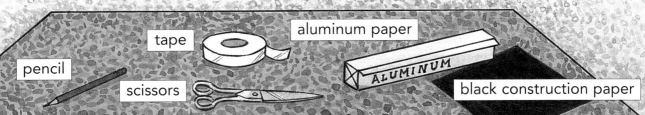

tape

aluminum paper

pencil

scissors

ALUMINUM

black construction paper

55
55

2 Take the black paper and place it so that one corner faces you.

3 Roll the black paper around the pencil.

HELP WINDOW

Asking for help

Can you give me a hand?

Please can you help me?

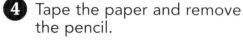

4 Tape the paper and remove the pencil.

5 Push both ends of the paper inside the tube.

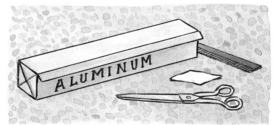

6 Measure and cut a piece of aluminum paper 60 X 40 mm.

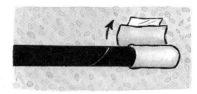

7 Roll the aluminum paper round one end of the tube and tape it.

Now you're ready for your first magic trick!

I can do that!

Josée and Maxim can do different magic tricks. Let's find out about them.

▶ Listen to Josée and Maxim talking.

▶ Check the tricks they can do.

▶ Put another check if they need help.

Abracadabra

HELP WINDOW

Expressing ability

Can you do a magic trick?

Yes, I can.

No, I can't.

Let the show begin!

To understand who someone is (1.1)

To understand polite forms for saying thank you, sorry (5.2)

At the beginning of the show, magicians introduce themselves. At the end, they thank the audience. Find out more.

► Listen to the magicians.

► Decide if they are introducing or thanking someone.

CLOSURE

You will understand and give information about your experiences and the experiences of people close to you. (1.0)

You will understand and give information related primarily to school life. (4.0)

You will understand and use the common expressions people use when they speak and write to each other. (5.0)

It's magic time! Are you ready? Let's go!

➤ Look at the list of things to do.
➤ Make sure you have everything you need.
➤ Get ready for the magic show.
➤ Have fun!

THINGS TO DO

1 Find a magic trick you can do.

2 Get the material you need for your trick.

3 Practise introducing yourself and your partner.

4 Practise thanking your audience.

5 Practise your trick.

This is what I learned.

1 I can introduce myself and my friend.

2 I can thank someone.

3 I can follow simple instructions.

I encouraged my partner.

I helped my partner.

Winter Fun!

skating

snowboarding

tobogganing

making a snowperson

making an angel in the snow

cross-country skiing

playing hockey in the street

sliding

going to a parade

going to a carnival

making sculptures

Brrr!
It's winter.

To understand what you must do (4.4)

Winter fun means winter parades!
Dress well—it's cold!

► Listen to Donna and Nadia.
► Find the clothes that Nadia needs.

HELP WINDOW

What are you wearing?

I'm wearing:

a tuque

a hat

I'm wearing:

a scarf

mittens

gloves

a coat

pants

a sweater

boots

leggings

running shoes and socks

Yes, I can!

To say what you can or cannot do (1.3)

Winter means outdoor fun! There are many things you can do!

► Name one activity you can do or one activity you cannot do.
► Write down the activity.

I can make a snowperson.

I can't ski.

HELP WINDOW

Can you? Can't you?

I'm a good skater.

I can skate so-so.

I can't ski well.

I can't ski at all.

Sure, I can skate.

I'm not a good skier.

Not really.

I can skate.

I can skate well.

Where do these sports come from?

To understand what a person or thing is (2.1)

Ice hockey, snowmobiling and skiing are all exciting winter sports. Do you know where they come from?

▸ Listen to the story of ice hockey, snowmobiling and skiing.

▸ Then listen to the questions.

▸ In your teams, answer the questions.

SKIING

SNOWMOBILING

ICE HOCKEY

Backyard fun

To understand instructions (4.1)

You can have a lot of fun right in your backyard! Have you ever tried to make a snow painting?

▶ Read how to make a snow painting.
▶ Put the illustrations in order.

How to make a snow painting

You need:

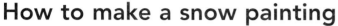

snow in the backyard

squeeze bottles

food colouring

a small shovel

water

a stick

A

B

C

D

Instructions

1. Flatten out a place in the snow. Use your hands or a shovel.

2. Draw something in the snow with the stick.

3. Mix food colouring and water in a squeeze bottle.

4. Use the colours to paint your drawing.

Optional: Last, spray clear water on the painting to preserve it.

You will understand and give information about your personal experiences and the experiences of people close to you. (1.0)

You will understand and give information about things outside your everyday life. (2.0)

You will understand and give information related primarily to school life. (4.0)

Winter is fun! Enter the Winter Fun poster contest.

▶ Choose a slogan.
▶ Read the poster contest rules.
▶ Make your poster.

Slogans

Winter can be fun!

Join in the fun!

Let's go out and play!

Winter Sports are great!

Snow, snow and more snow!

Contest rules

1. Draw a winter scene.
2. Include winter activities.
3. Make it original.
4. Use colours.
5. Write a slogan.

This is what I learned.

1 **Can you do these activities?**

2 **Can you answer the questions?**

Who invented the snowmobile?
Where did ice hockey start?
What sport was invented in Sweden?

3 **Can you understand the instructions?**

1. Make a large snowball
2. Make a medium snowball.
   Put it on the large ball.
3. Make another small snowball.
   Put it on the medium ball. That's the head.
4. Use stones to make eyes and a nose.
5. Use red food colouring to make a mouth.
6. Paint blue buttons on the body.
7. Put a hat and a warm scarf on the head.

What have you got?

Did I
participate?

Did I let others
give their ideas?

Did I listen to
others?

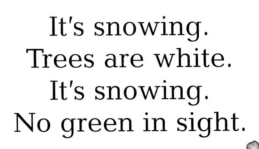

Snow

It's snowing.
Trees are white.
It's snowing.
No green in sight.

It's snowing.
Animal tracks.
It's snowing.
Crack, crack.

It's snowing.
Darkness is creeping
It's snowing.
Nature is sleeping. Zzzz . . .

It's snowing.

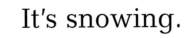

Jenny Lives on Hunter Street

**ACTIVITY 1**

Where are you?

To give a factual description of a person, an animal, an event, an object or a place (2.2)

There are many places around town. Can you describe them?

► Think of a yes/no question to ask about the places.

► Ask a yes/no question to find out where you are.

school

fire station

library

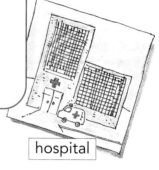
hospital

bank

post office

police station

small shopping centre

HELP WINDOW

Yes/No questions

Do you read books here?

No, you don't.

Do you eat here?

Yes, you do.

Jenny lives on Hunter Street.

To understand the major elements of a
story: characters, conflict, events (3.1)

Finding Jenny's house is easy, if you
know the way.

▶ Listen to the story.
▶ Write down all the ideas you can
remember from the story.

Jenny can't come to my house.
Jenny can't come to play.
Jenny can't come to my house.
She doesn't know the way.

Mum, can I play at Jenny's house
If her Mum says it's OK?
Mum, can we walk to Jenny's house?
I'm sure I know the way.

Jenny lives on Hunter Street,
And I live by the Bay.
It isn't far to Hunter Street.
I think I know the way.

We need to walk down Bay Street,
Along the right-hand side,
And then across the little park,
Where I play on the slide.

Past the pond where the ducks are
And through the tall green gate,
And here we are on Hunter Street.
The number's forty-eight.

Now Jenny can
come to my house—
Maybe next
Saturday?
Jenny can come
to my house.
The map shows
her the way.

Jenny and me

To compare the world of a story, and
yourself and your own experiences (3.3)

Jenny lives on Hunter Street. Where
do you live?

▶ Read the facts about Jenny from the
story.

▶ Write down the same information
about yourself.

Jenny lives on Hunter Street.

I live on Bay Street.

JENNY

- Hunter Street
- Number 48
- across the park

ME

_____Street

That's where Jenny lives.

To understand how to get to a certain place (4.3)

Can you find Jenny's house? Do you know the way?

▶ Listen to the story a second time.
▶ Trace the way to Jenny's house.

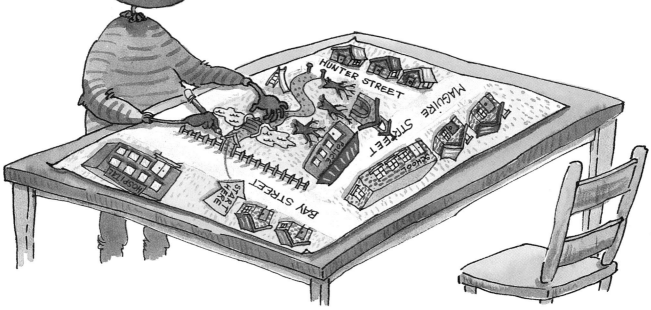

HELP WINDOW

Direction words

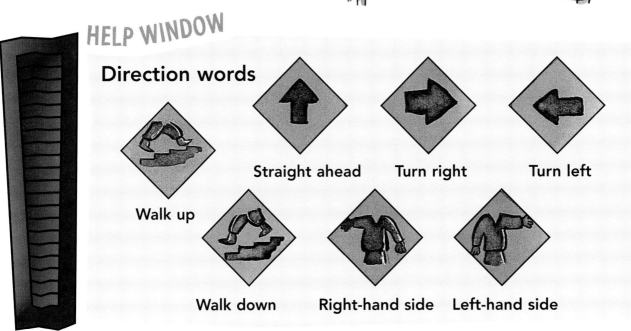

Walk up   Straight ahead   Turn right   Turn left

Walk down   Right-hand side   Left-hand side

Can you find me?

To tell someone how to get to a certain place (4.3)

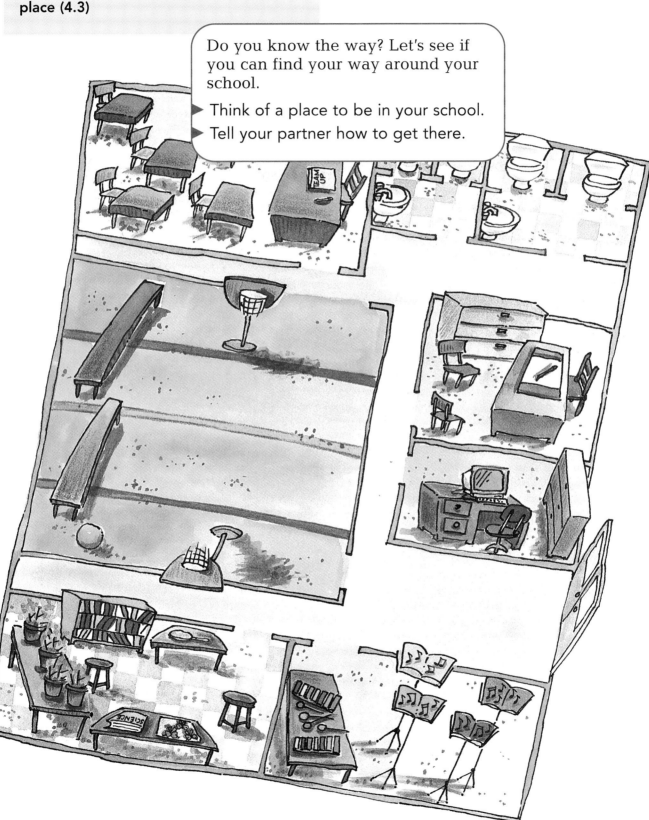

Do you know the way? Let's see if you can find your way around your school.

► Think of a place to be in your school.
► Tell your partner how to get there.

I live on Magic Street.

You will understand a story and react to it. (3.0)

You will understand and give information about activities related primarily to school life. (4.0)

New ideas, new story. Why not make up your own story?

▶ Choose a new character and new places.

▶ Write your own story.

Check-up TIME

This is what I learned.

1 I can name lots of places.

2 Do you . . .

eat in a library?

sleep in a restaurant?

go shopping at the police station?

3 Do you know the way to the fire station?

I took turns in my team.

I helped my partners.

I listened to others talk.

I'm happy about my team's work.

Can you find your way on a map?

☞ Choose two places.

☞ Tell your friend how to get from one place to the other place.

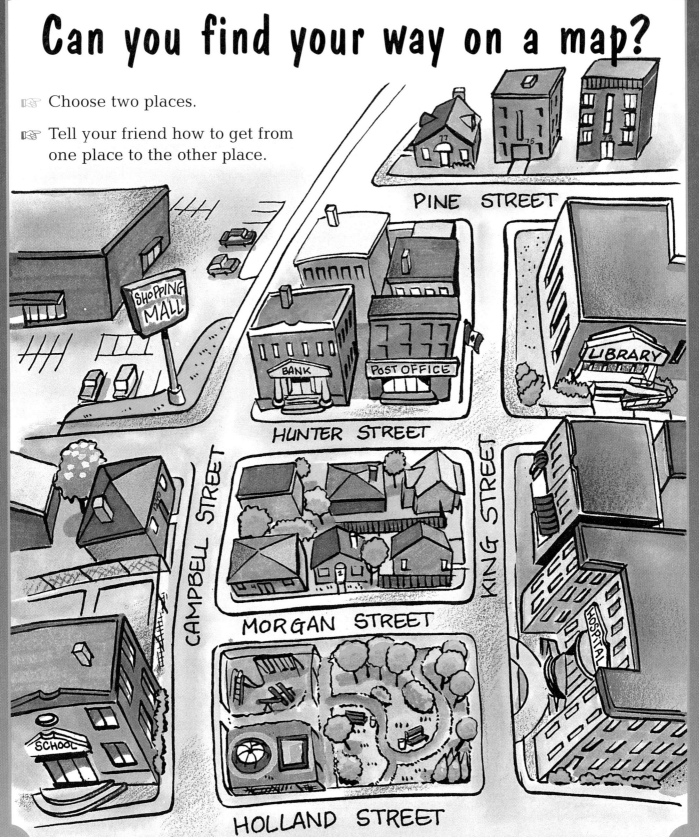

The Inventor

A magazine about inventions and inventors

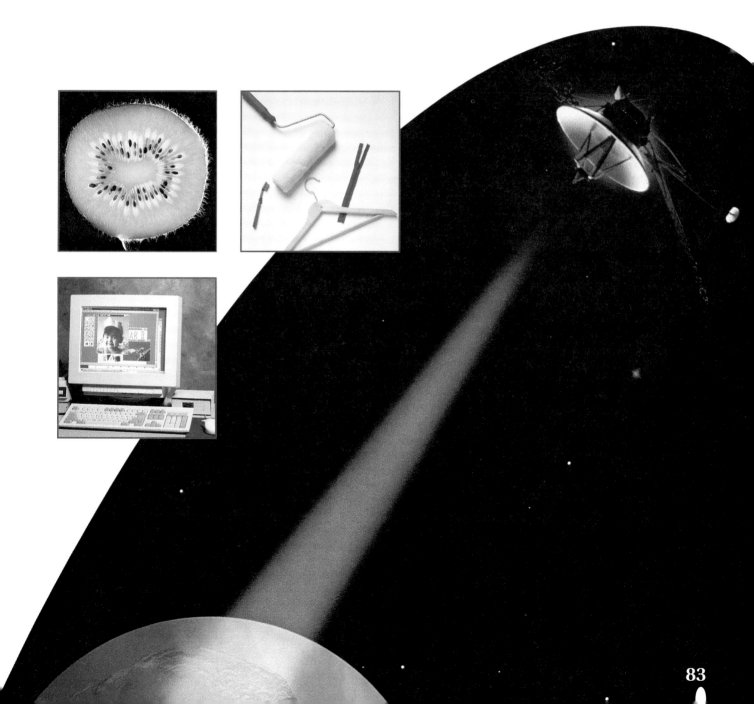

Check it out!

To say what you can or cannot do (1.3)

So many objects, so many inventions! Can you find these inventions at home?

▶ Look at the inventions.

▶ Tell your teammates whether you can find them at home.

▶ Do you know who invented them?

basketball and net

skate

paint roller

snowmobile

light bulb

dial telephone

Robertson screws

Inventors: basketball: James Naismith; **paint roller:** Norman Breakey; **screws:** Peter Robertson; **snowmobile:** Armand Bombardier; **telephone:** Alexander Bell; **light bulb:** Thomas Edison; **ice skates:** John Forbes

Mothers of invention

To understand what a person or thing is
(2.1)

> Inventors and inventions! Let's find out who invented what.
> ▶ Listen to the inventor.
> ▶ Identify her invention.
> ▶ Write down the name of the inventor and her invention.

Laura Robinson

Olivia Poole

Bette Nesmith Graham

Ruth Wakefield

CORRECTION FLUID

ABSOLUTE BALDERDASH GAME

Unusual uses

> To give a report about a person, an animal, an event, an object or a place (2.3)

Some inventions may have different uses. Can you think of some?

➤ Think of an unusual use for each object.

➤ Draw and name your invention.

➤ Tell another team about your ideas.

Invention
Whiz Quiz!

To understand a factual description of a person, an animal, an event, an object or a place (2.2)

To understand polite forms for saying thank you, sorry (5.2)

Do our Invention Whiz Quiz!

▶ Read each clue. What invention does it describe?

▶ Check your answers with your partner.

▶ Complete the puzzle.

HELP WINDOW

Taking turns

Now it's your turn.

What do you think?

Thanks for your help.

Sorry about that.

Excuse me, it's your turn.

Thank you, now it's your turn.

You will understand and produce simple messages about your personal experiences and the experiences of people close to you. (1.0)

You will understand and give information about things outside your everyday life. (2.0)

Now it's your turn to be an inventor!

▶ Think of an invention.
▶ Draw your own version of it.
▶ Say what it can do.

Check-up TIME

This is what I learned.

1 I can name five new inventions in my home.

2 I know who invented these things.

3 I can name an old invention and its inventor.

I took turns in my team.

I was polite to my teammates.

I helped my teammates.

Invention name game

Name an invention that begins with the letter C.
Name an invention that is good to eat.
Name an invention you have in your bedroom.
Name an invention you can find in space.
Name an invention that makes a noise.
Name an invention you use at school.
Name an old invention.
Name a new invention.
Name an invention made of plastic.
Name an invention that goes in the water.

Snack Time

milk

spoon

bowl

measuring cup

butter

whip

sugar

plate

flour

pan

eggs

breakfast

lunch and dinner

supper

snack

Food survey

To say what you like, dislike, want or prefer (1.2)

Some foods we like. Some foods we dislike. Find out about your classmates' tastes.

▶ Look at the drawings.
▶ Ask your classmates questions.
▶ Write their answers on the questionnaire.

HELP WINDOW

Do you like to eat . . .?

Do you like to drink . . .?

Do you like . . .?

What's in your lunch box?

**To understand what a person or thing is
(2.1)**

> It's now time to discover what your friends put in their lunch boxes. Is it a good lunch or not? You be the judge.
>
> ► Guess what's in the lunch boxes.
> ► Listen to the students and see if you are right.

97

Your favourite snack

To give instructions (4.1)

We all have a favourite snack. Why don't you share yours!

▶ Write a short recipe for your favourite snack.

My favourite food is a tomato sandwich. The ingredients are tomato, bread, butter, mayonnaise, lettuce, salt and pepper. Here's how you make it.

1. Cut the tomato into slices.

2. Toast two slices of bread.

3. Spread butter and mayonnaise on the toasted bread.

4. Put the tomato and lettuce on one of the slices of toast.

5. Add a pinch of salt and pepper. Put the other slice on top. Lunch is served!

HELP WINDOW

take

add

pour

cook

measure

mix, stir

CLOSURE

You will understand and give information about your personal experiences and the experiences of people close to you. (1.0)

You will understand and give information about things outside your everyday life. (2.0)

You will understand and give information about activities related primarily to school life. (4.0)

RECIPE: _____
INGREDIENTS: _____

INSTRUCTIONS: _____
1. _____
2. _____
3. _____
4. _____
5. _____
6. _____

Food groups: Put a check mark next to the food groups included in your recipe.
☐ Fruits and vegetables   ☐ Meat
☐ Bread and cereals   ☐ Dairy products

Now it's time for you to make your classroom cookbook.

▶ Write down your recipe.
▶ Check (✔) the food groups.
▶ Put the recipes together to make a class recipe book.

RECIPE: _____
INGREDIENTS: _____

INSTRUCTIONS: _____
1. _____
2. _____
3. _____
4. _____
5. _____
6. _____

Food groups: Put a check mark next to the food groups included in your recipe.
Fruits and vegetables   ☐ Meat
☐ Dairy products

Check-up TIME

This is what I learned.

I can talk about my favourite food.

I can name foods in their food groups.

I can write simple instructions for a recipe.

I can describe the foods in my lunch box.

I can say which foods make a healthy lunch.

I participated enthusiastically.

I contributed my ideas.

Mischievous Sam

Practical jokes

bucket of water

giggling

spraying

Too messy

Too difficult

frog

spider

Story time: part one

To understand the major elements of a story: characters, conflict, events (3.1)

Here's Sam and her family. What's happening?

▶ Listen to part one of the story "Mischievous Sam".

▶ Cut out the illustrations and paste them on the flow chart.

Sam and her family

Ha! Ha!

ACTIVITY 2

Story time: part two

To understand a description of the major elements of a story: characters, conflict, events (3.2)

To understand idioms and fixed expressions (5.4)

Not all jokes are funny. Some practical jokes can be dangerous and messy.

▶ Listen to part two of the story.
▶ Decide if the jokes are **dangerous**, **difficult**, **messy** or **O.K.**

Here's the spider.

Early in the morning . . .

That's enough!

HELP WINDOW

Common expressions

What happens next?

To describe the major elements of a
story: characters, conflict, events (3.2)

Sam's family think of many practical
jokes. Not all of them are funny.

▶ Look at the picture and describe what
you see.
▶ Think of a joke to play on Sam.

*So they put a plastic
snake in Sam's bed.*

Watch out!

To understand a warning or caution (4.5)

To give a warning or caution (4.5)

Some practical jokes aren't safe.
- Look at the practical jokes.
- Decide which ones are dangerous.
- Tell your teammates what you think.

ACTIVITY

5

Who
is like me?

**To understand comparisons between the
world of a story, and yourself and your
own experiences (3.3)**

Sometimes we think and act like
characters in a story. Who are you like
in "Mischievous Sam" ?

▶ Listen to the whole story.

▶ Choose the character who is most like
you.

Making my own book

To understand instructions (4.1)

> Would you like to have your own book about Mischievous Sam? Here's how to make one.
>
> ▶ Read the instructions.
> ▶ Make your own book.

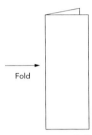

Step 1: Fold the page like a hot-dog bun.

Step 2: Open the page.

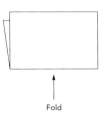

Step 3: Fold the page like a hamburger bun.

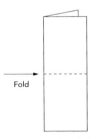

Step 4: Fold the page like a hot-dog bun again.

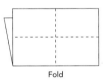

Step 5: Open the fold made in step 4.

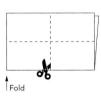

Step 6: With the fold at the bottom, cut a slit.

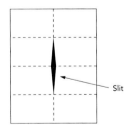

Step 7: Open up the page.

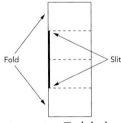

Step 8: Fold the page like a hot-dog bun.

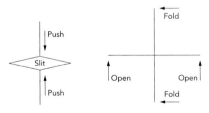

Step 9: Push, fold, open.

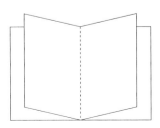

Step 10: Fold the pages so that you make a book. Make sure the covers are on the outside!

You will understand a story and react to it. (3.0)

You will understand and give information about activities related primarily to school life. (4.0)

Every good book has a good ending. How does your story end?

▶ Write your favourite ending on the last page of your own mini-book.

▶ Make sure the joke is safe.

▶ Illustrate the end of the story.

▶ Colour in your picture.

NONE OF HER SOCKS MATCHED!

Check-up TIME

This is what I learned.

1 I can name all the characters.

2 I can describe what happened.

3 I can understand the instructions.

| Fold | Cut | Write | Push | Draw |

Sports Sensations

walking

swimming

in-line skating

baseball

soccer

cycling

field hockey

gymnastics

running

badminton

Sports for everyone

To understand what someone can or cannot do (1.3)

There's a sport for everyone. Find out what different sports students can do.

▶ Listen to four students talk about the sports they play.

▶ In your teams, answer your teacher's questions.

HELP WINDOW

I'm able to . . .   I can . . .

run

play

hit

skate

throw

catch

swim

Something different

To understand a report about a person,
an animal, an event, an object or a place
(2.3)

Do you like to try different sports?
Find out about three new ones.

▶ Listen to some students talk about
their sports.

▶ Match the sport with its illustration.
Write down the correct letter.

What do you think?

To give a report about a person, an animal, an event, an object or a place (2.3)

Which sports are the most exciting?

▶ Pick a card.

▶ Name the sport on the card and say what you think about it.

This is water skiing. It looks exciting, don't you think?

I think it's cool.

Yes it does.

Not me!

HELP WINDOW

It looks exciting.

It sounds sensational.

I think it's difficult.

Wow!

Breathtaking!

It sounds great.

It looks dangerous.

Nervous, sad, happy?

To understand how someone feels and what someone is going to do (1.5)

To understand idioms and fixed expressions (5.4)

Before and after a competition, athletes feel many different things.

▶ Listen to the athletes.
▶ Write down how they feel.
▶ In the help window, find the expression that matches each feeling.

HELP WINDOW

I'm scared stiff.

I've got butterflies in my stomach.

I'm as happy as a lark.

CLOSURE

You will understand and give information about your personal experiences and experiences of people close to you. (1.0)

You will understand and give information about things outside your everyday life. (2.0)

Play the sports sensations game. May the best player win!

▶ Form teams of four.
▶ Play the game.

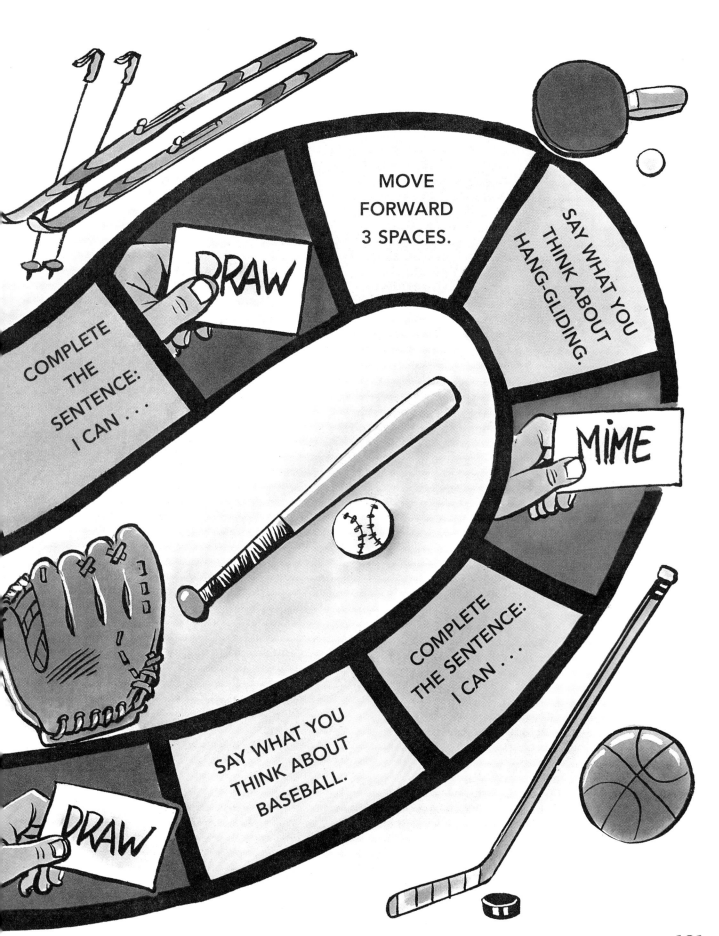

MOVE FORWARD 3 SPACES.

SAY WHAT YOU THINK ABOUT HANG-GLIDING.

DRAW

COMPLETE THE SENTENCE: I CAN . . .

MIME

COMPLETE THE SENTENCE: I CAN . . .

SAY WHAT YOU THINK ABOUT BASEBALL.

DRAW

Check-up TIME

This is what I learned.

1 I can say which sports I can play.

2 I know these expressions.

I'm scared stiff.

I'm full of beans.

I've got butterflies in my stomach.

I'm as happy as a lark.

3 I can describe the sports I play.

I talked quietly.

I took turns with my teammates.

Bike Safety

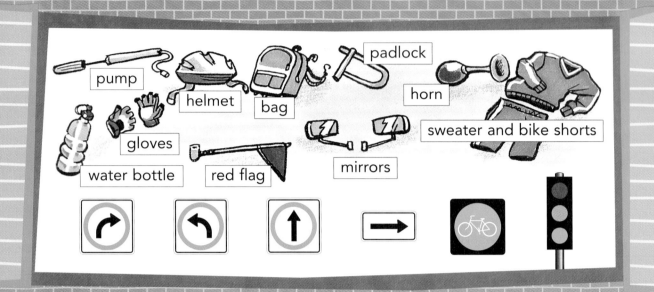

ACTIVITY 1

What kind of cyclist are you?

To understand what someone can or cannot do (1.3)

What kind of cyclist are you? Find out by answering the quiz.

▶ Look at the pictures.
▶ Talk about what you see.
▶ Listen to your teacher.

Accessories

To understand what someone likes,
dislikes, wants or prefers (1.2)

It's important to have some accessories for your safety. Are there any accessories you want in particular? What do you think it is important to have?

▶ Listen carefully to the students talking.

▶ What accessories do they think are important? Write them down.

We're going to prepare for our bicycle safety week.

What are we going to do?

We'll make our own bicycle safety brochure.

Mr Thomson, are we going to talk about accessories?

Yes. Come and look at the things on the table.

Traffic signs

To say what you or someone else must do (4.4)

Road signs are for everyone. Cyclists have special signs. Here are some of them.

► Look at the traffic signs.

► Test your knowledge by playing a flashcard game.

Flashcard game.

127

Safety rules

To understand a warning (4.5)

Do, Should

Don't, Shouldn't

There are rules for drivers and rules for cyclists! Find out about some of them.

▶ Listen to the tape.

▶ Associate the correct picture with the rule.

Oh! Excuse me!

CLOSURE

You will understand and give information about your personal experiences and the experiences of people close to you. (1.0)

You will understand and give information about activities related primarily to school life. (4.0)

Show other students what you know about bicycle safety.

▶ Read the instructions.
▶ Make sure you understand what to do.
▶ Pair up with your partner.
▶ Make your own bicycle safety brochure.

1. Make sure you have all the necessary information for your brochure.
2. Write neatly and clearly.

Check-up TIME

This is what I learned.

1 I can name the accessories I need.

2 I know what I must do when I see these signs.

3 I can understand *Do* rules and *Don't* rules.

I shared ideas with my partners.

I encouraged my partners.

I listened well.

The Case of the Missing Person

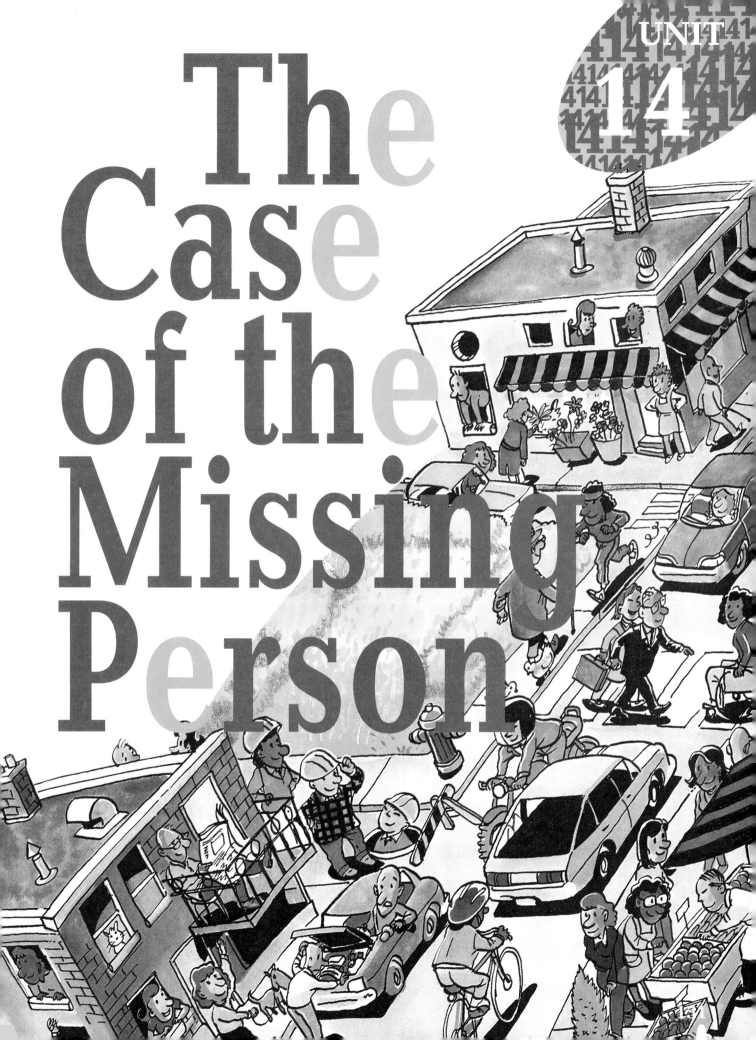

DETECTIVE JONES MR BERNSTEIN MS BERNSTEIN

telephone notepad pencil magnifying glass

What colour is her hair?

What is she wearing?

How old is she?

What's her name?

What colour are her eyes?

The case of the missing person, part one

To understand the major elements of a story: characters, conflict, events (3.1)

Find out about Mr Bernstein's problem.

Listen carefully to the conversation.

Answer your teacher's questions.

2 What's the problem?

To understand what a person or thing is (2.1)

To understand someone who asks for help (4.2)

Help the police fill in the form about Mr Bernstein's call.

▶ Copy the police form in your note-book.

▶ Listen to the conversation. Fill in the missing information.

POLICE DEPARTMENT

Date: _____

Caller's family name: _____

Caller's first name: _____

Address: _____

_____

_____

Reason for the call: _____

ACTIVITY 3

The case of the missing person, part two

To understand a description of the major elements of a story: characters, conflict, events (3.2)

Someone's missing. What does she look like?

▶ Listen to the story carefully.
▶ Fill in the ID card.

Is this really Ms Bernstein?

To understand a factual description of a person, an animal, an event, an object or a place (2.2)

Are you ready to play the role of the police artist?

► Read the questions.
► Look at the information written in your notebook.
► Draw Ms Bernstein's face.
► Colour it in.

What colour is her hair?

Is it short?

Is it long?

Is it curly?

Is it straight?

What colour are her eyes?

Does she have a small nose?

Is her nose pointed?

What colour are her lips?

The case of the missing person, part three

To understand the major elements of a story: characters, conflict, events (3.1)

What do you think will happen next?

- Listen carefully to the story.
- Guess the ending.
- Share your ideas with your partner.

Your emergency guidelines

You will understand and give information about your personal experiences and the experiences of people close to you. (1.0)

You will understand and give information about things outside your everyday life. (2.0)

What are you supposed to do in an emergency?

▶ Write down information about yourself.

1. Whom to call or notify in an emergency

Police telephone number: _____

Friend's name and telephone number: _____

Parent's or guardian's name and work number: _____

Relative's name and telephone number: _____

2. Information about yourself

Name: _____

Parent's or guardian's name: _____

Address: _____

Colour of hair: _____

Colour of eyes: _____

Height: _____

Distinguishing features: _____

IMPORTANT!

Don't leave home without telling someone.

Write a note.

Phone your parents at work.

Tell a friend.

Call a relative.

Check-up TIME

This is what I learned.

1 I can identify the main characters.

2 I can understand the description of a person.

3 I know whom to call in an emergency.

1. Whom to call or notify in an emergency

Police telephone number:

Friend's name and telephone number:

Parent's or guardian's name and work number:

Relative's name and telephone number:

4 I know what to do in an emergency.

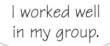

I worked well in my group.

I listened actively in my group.

140

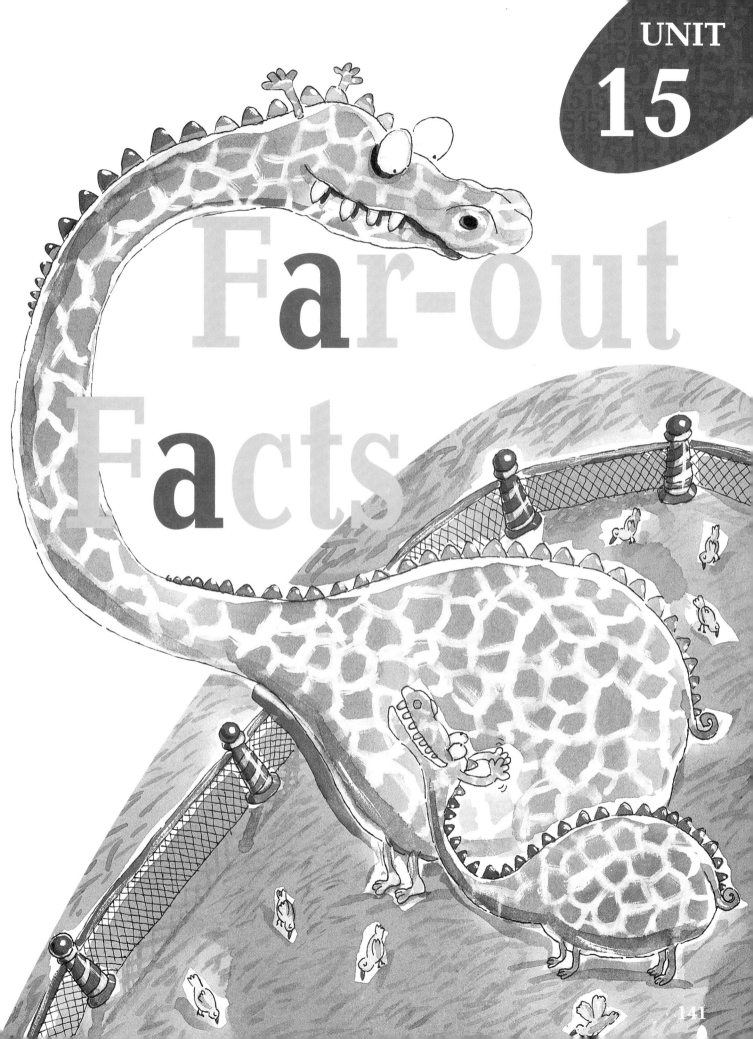

Far-out
Facts

world

plane

bees

snowperson

hive

owl

snake

tongue

giraffes

dinosaurs

What do you know?

To understand a factual description of a person, an animal, an event, an object or a place (2.2)

Can you find the facts?

> Listen to the facts.
> Find the matching illustration.

1

2

3

HELP WINDOW

tall → taller → tallest
big → bigger → biggest
large → larger → largest
small → smaller → smallest
short → shorter → shortest

4

Are you fact-wise?

If you had 3 or 4 correct matches: Congratulations! You're fact-wise.

If you had 0 to 2 correct matches: Great try! Stay tuned for more facts.

Amazing animal facts

To understand what a person or thing is (2.1)

Animals do surprising things. Let's look at the facts.

▶ Read the text.
▶ Find the facts.

1 Did you know that most giraffes have dark tongues? That's right! Animals' tongues are usually pink. What colour is your tongue?

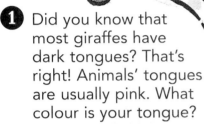

2 Some birds have large eyes. Their big eyes help them to find food. But do you know that their eyes do not move? Birds have to move their heads and turn their necks to see everything. Try it.

3 Did you know that a snake's tongue is not dangerous? A snake doesn't have a nose. It uses its tongue to feel and smell things. Awesome!

4 Bees dance to keep warm. The bees make a group. They move their bodies. They move their wings very fast. The movements produce heat. It warms their bodies and their hive.

Dinostory

**To understand the major elements of a
story: characters, conflict, events (3.1)**

What really happened to the
dinosaurs?

➤ Listen to the story.

➤ Draw a picture of part of the story.

➤ Present your picture to your teammates.

*What happened to
the dinosaurs?*

A long time ago . . .

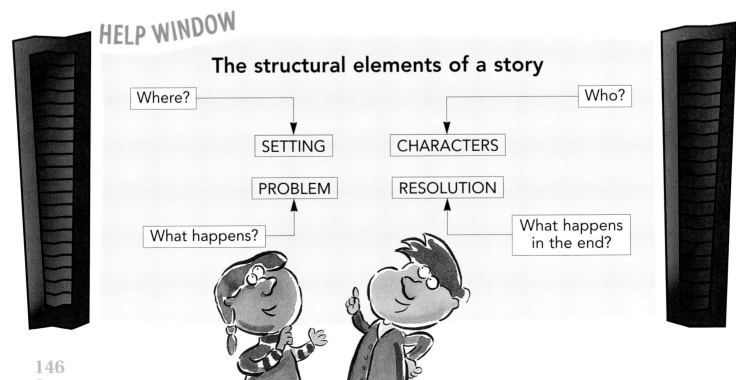

HELP WINDOW

The structural elements of a story

Where? →		Who? ↓
	SETTING	CHARACTERS
	PROBLEM	RESOLUTION
What happens? ↑		What happens in the end?

ACTIVITY 4 · Dinosaur world

To understand a report about a person,
an animal, an event, an object or a place
(2.3)

> Amy went on holiday. Find out what she saw.
>
> ▶ Listen to Amy.
> ▶ Write down the numbers of the things she saw.

WELCOME TO DINOSAUR WORLD

❶ ❷ ❸ ❹ ❺ ❻

What's that fact?

To say what a person, an animal, an event, an object or a place is (2.1)

To give a factual description of a person, an animal, an event, an object or a place (2.2)

To ask someone to give you information or to explain something (5.3)

Can you remember what you learned?

▶ Read the What's that fact? questions.
▶ Write the answers on the puzzle.
▶ Find the hidden word.

Please say that again.

Sure.

Ready to play the Far-Out Fact game?

To understand instructions (4.1)

To understand someone who asks for help (4.2)

Everyone can play the Far-Out Fact game! But first you must prepare it.

> Cut out the cube.
> Fold the cube on the dotted lines.
> Tape the edges together.
> Cut out the game cards.

Game rules

You need a set of question cards, a die and four players.

Instructions

1. Place the question cards face down.
2. Number each player from 1 to 4.
3. Player 1 throws the die.
4. If your number is on the die, pick a card. Read the question to the team and answer it.
5. The other players decide if the answer is correct or not.
6. If the die says "Ask a question", you must ask your teammate a question. If the die says "Miss your turn", go on to the next player.
7. Player 2 throws the die. Repeat steps 4 to 6.
8. Play the game until there are no more question cards.

Points

Give one point for every correct answer. The team with the most points is the winner.

Play the Far-Out Fact game!

You will understand and give information about things outside your everyday life. (2.0)

You will understand and give simple messages about activities related primarily to school life (4.0)

You will understand and use the common expressions people use when they speak and write to each other. (5.0)

It's fun-fact time. How fact-wise are you?

Play the game.

Do you understand what to do?

How do snakes smell?

Great answer!

Let's continue. Throw the die.

151

Check-up TIME

This is what I learned.

1. I learned some new facts.

2. I can tell my partner two facts about dinosaurs.

3. I know what happened to dinosaurs.

I encouraged my teammates.

I helped my teammates.

Cirque du Soleil

Come one, come all!

To understand an invitation or a suggestion (4.6)

> Come to a special event!
> ▶ Listen to the message.
> ▶ Fill in the poster.

Where? When? Who?

HELP WINDOW

Where → **a place**

Where are you going?   To the cinema.

Who → **a person**

Who's your English teacher?   Louise.

When → **a date, season, time**

When is your birthday?   October 17.

ACTIVITY 2

Discover Cirque du Soleil

To give a factual description of a person, an animal, an event, an object or a place (2.2)

Have you ever seen the blue and yellow big top? Do you know anything about Cirque du Soleil?

► Look at the pictures.
► Share your ideas with your classmates.

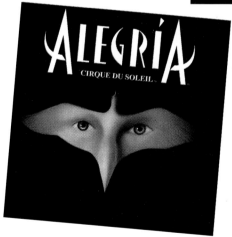

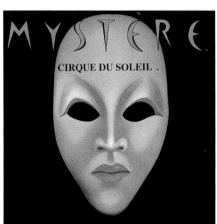

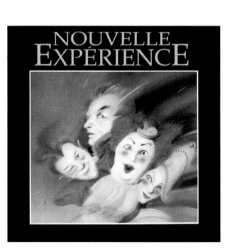

Guy Laliberté

CIRQUE DU SOLEIL
1984

Montréal, Sainte-Foy, Toronto, Vancouver, Paris, Las Vegas, Los Angeles, San Francisco, Japan and Germany

To understand what a person, an animal,
an event, an object or a place is (2.1)

To say what a person, an animal, an
event, an object or a place is (2.1)

Learn more about Cirque du Soleil's
show *Quidam*.

▶ Read what the newspapers say.
▶ Share the information with your
partners.

Cirque du Soleil presents its new show, QUIDAM.

Quidam has been presented in many cities, including Santa Monica and Costa Mesa.

It premiered in Montréal on 23 April, 1996.

CIRQUE DU SOLEIL'S GREAT SHOW QUIDAM

There are forty-two artists.

The artists come from many different countries — Canada, Russia, China, France, the United States, Austria and Switzerland.

Singing is part of the music for the show.

People around the world love Cirque du Soleil.

It's just magical!

One great big family

To understand an introduction to another person or when someone says hello or goodbye (5.1)

Cirque du Soleil has many artists. There are also important people behind the scenes. Come and meet some of them.

▶ Listen to the recording.

▶ Draw the grid in your notebooks.

▶ Write down what each person does at the circus.

CLOSURE

You will understand and give information about things outside your everyday life. (2.0)

Put your ideas together and create a collage on Cirque du Soleil.

▶ Create your collage.
▶ Share your work with your classmates.

CIRQUE DU SOLEIL

This is our poster. Here is an acrobat.

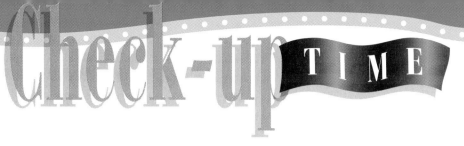

Check-up TIME

This is what I learned.

1 I can understand an invitation.

2 I can talk about Cirque du Soleil.

Places visited

Performers

Names of shows

> I talked when it was my turn.

> I listened well.

The circus game

Now that you are an expert on Cirque du Soleil,
have fun playing the circus card game.

RULES

❶ Play in groups of four.

What's the name of
the circus?

❷ Pick a card.

**❸ Read the question to the student
on your left.**

Hurry, you only
have 15 seconds
to answer.

**❹ Give your teammate one minute to
answer.**

**❺ At the end of the game, count up
the points.**

Let's Vacation

Hey, it's vacation time.

To say how you feel and what you are going to do (1.5)

The summer vacation is near. What do you plan to do?

▶ Interview your teammate about his or her summer plans.

▶ Share your teammate's answer with the rest of the group.

HELP WINDOW

Questions

What are you going to do this summer?

What do you plan to do this summer?

Do you have vacation plans?

Ways to respond

I'm going to visit my grandparents.

I don't have plans yet.

Not really.

I'm not sure yet.

I don't know.

I plan to swim every day.

What can you do in your neighbourhood?

To understand who someone is (1.1)

To understand what someone can or cannot do (1.3)

Let's find out what other young people can do in their town.

▶ Listen to the young people.

▶ Write the name of the person, the place they live, and the activities they do.

▶ If you can do the activity in your neighbourhood, check it off.

How about a day camp?

To understand a suggestion or an invitation (4.6)

To say what you like, dislike, want or prefer (1.2)

Summer day camps are fun. Let's go!

Part one
▶ Listen to Nadine's suggestions.
▶ Match the suggestion to the correct day.

Part two
▶ Decide which activity you prefer.
▶ Share your answer with your team-mates.

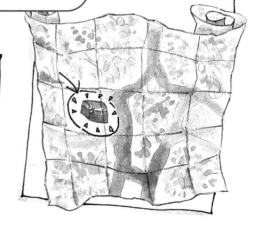

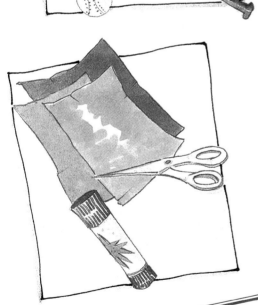

Come to the English Day Camp.
Every week, July and August
Ages 8 to 12
Register now!

Places to visit

To understand what a person, an animal, a thing, an event or a place is (2.1)

Do you like to travel? Here are some places to go with your family.

▶ Listen to the commercials for the places you can visit.

▶ Choose the matching illustration.

▶ Write the letter in your notebook.

It's my vacation.

To say what you like, dislike, want or prefer (1.2)

> There are so many things to do! What do you like to do?
>
> ➤ Think of activities you and your teammates like to do.
>
> ➤ Share your ideas with your teammates.
>
> ➤ Find other classmates who like the same activities.

You will understand and give information about your personal experiences and the experiences of people close to you. (1.0)

You will understand and give information about activities related primarily to school life. (4.0)

What to do? Where to go? What's your ideal vacation?

▶ Work with your team. Think of an ideal place to visit.

▶ Think of activities to do.

▶ Make a collage of your ideal vacation.

This is what I learned.

Do you have summer plans?

Can you go to the library?

What activities do you like to do in the summer?

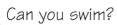
Can you swim?

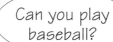
Can you play baseball?

Can you do arts and crafts?

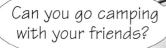
Can you go camping with your friends?

Can you suggest three activities to your friend?

I listened to my teammates.

I shared my ideas and opinions.

My team was able to make decisions.

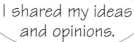

Same or different?

Songs

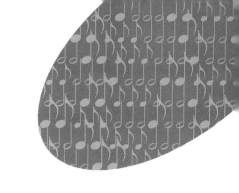

How are you today?

Hello, how are you today?
Everybody say
       "Hello, how are you today?"
I'm so pleased to meet you.
I'm happy to be with you.
Hello, how are you today?

Goodbye, so long, see you soon.
Bye-bye, so long, see you soon.
Must go now, see you later.
Got to leave now, alligator.
Goodbye, so long, see you soon.

Good morning, boys and girls,
How are you?
Good afternoon, boys and girls,
How are you?
It's great to be here,
So nice to be near.
Hello, boys and girls,
How are you?

Months and days

January, February, March, April and May,
June, July, August, September
All have beautiful days.
October, November and December
Are nice in their way.
Now that we know the months of the year,
Let's all learn the days.

Monday, Tuesday, Wednesday, Thursday, Friday
Are all weekdays.
Saturday, Sunday, Saturday, Sunday
Are my favourite days.
Monday, Tuesday, Wednesday, Thursday and Friday
Are all school days.
Now that we know the days of the week,
Hey, guys, what do we say? We say,

O.K. ALL TOGETHER NOW:

Monday, Tuesday, Wednesday, Thursday, Friday
Are all weekdays.
Saturday, Sunday, Saturday, Sunday
Are my favourite days.
Monday, Tuesday, Wednesday, Thursday, Friday,
Saturday and Sunday.
Now that we know the days and the months,
Let's go out and play.

175

Numbers

One plus one is two.

This is what we can do.

Two plus one is three,

Come and dance with me.

Three plus one is four,

Everyone stand on the floor.

Four plus one is five,

Wave your hands, people arrive.

I know my numbers:

1, 2, 3, 4, 5.

I know my numbers:

Have fun counting to five.

Six plus one is seven,

Flap your arms like a chicken.

Seven plus one is eight,

Make a smile: you look great.

Eight plus one is nine,

Don't stop, you look so fine.

Nine plus one is ten,

Let's all sing it again.

I know my numbers:

6, 7, 8, 9, 10.

I know my numbers:

I can count up to ten.

Colours

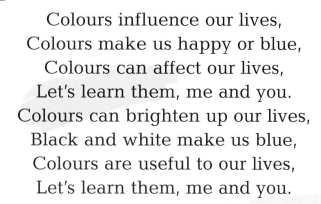

Colours influence our lives,
Colours make us happy or blue,
Colours can affect our lives,
Let's learn them, me and you.
Colours can brighten up our lives,
Black and white make us blue,
Colours are useful to our lives,
Let's learn them, me and you.

We've got green for the grass that grows all summer,
Yellow for the leaves in the fall,
White for the snow that stays all winter,
Hey! And that's not all.
We've got gray for the spring when the snow melts,
Blue for the sky up above,
Red for a setting sunset,
Now we can sing all about . . .

Colours! Green, yellow and white.
Colours! Gray, blue and red.
Colours are coming my way.
Colours! Black , orange and gold.
Colours! Silver, brown, violet.
Colours! Let's learn them today.

We've got black for the night when it's dark out,
Orange is the fruit that we eat,
Gold is for a precious metal,
Hey! What do you think?
Silver for a quarter we buy with,
Brown for the earth that we dig,
Violet is a beautiful flower,
Now we can sing all about . . .

SONG 5 · Family love

If you have love within your family,
Love you are willing to share,
Respect within the family
Will come if you really care.
Patience with the people in your family.
Treat them with love and care,
And the love that you find
Will last to the end of time,
For when you love, love will be there.

SONG 6 · Magic

Do you believe in a magic tree?
Do you believe in what you see?
Birds that appear from nowhere,
People who come from nowhere.

Do you believe in magic?
Do you believe in what you see?
Do you believe in magic?
Will you believe it when you see
Tricks done for you and me?
Magic . . . Magic . . .

Do you believe in magic cards,
Tricks that are easy, tricks that are hard?
Do you believe in a magic act,
Pulling out rabbits from a hat?

Do you believe in a magic show?
Do you see? Do you know?
Do you believe in magic sticks?
Do you like to play some tricks?

Doing the Body Twist

Put your hands in the air and make them do the Twist.

Move your fingers in the air and make them do the Twist.

Swing your arms in the air and do the Body Twist.

Put your finger on your nose and turn it round and round.

Put your hand on your mouth and blow everyone a kiss.

Blink your eyes at a person and do the Body Twist.

We're doing the Body Twist!

We're doing the Body Twist!

Shake your shoulders in a Body Twist,

Move your legs in a Body Twist,

Close your eyes, rub your ears,

Jump to your feet, point your toes.

Everybody's doing the Body Twist!

Bend your knees, draw a circle

And move them round and round.

Now move your hips in a circle

And move them round and round.

Twist your body in a circle

And do the Body Twist!

179

Going on vacation

What are you doing on vacation,
Doing on vacation?
I am gonna have fun.
Are you going on vacation,
Going on vacation?
Yes and I'm gonna have fun.

I'm going horseback riding with Mom and Dad,
Going on a fishing trip won't be sad,
I'll play some baseball, soccer and some hockey too
And yes I'm gonna have fun.

I'm going with my mother to P.E.I.
Playing in the ocean, my oh my!
I'll see my cousins, aunts and uncles, hi hi hi!
And yes I'm gonna have fun.

What are we doing on vacation,
Doing on vacation?
We are gonna have fun.
Are we going on vacation,
Going on vacation?
Yes and we're gonna have fun.

We'll stay at home, watch TV every day,
Don't have no projects anyway.
We'll spend the rest of the summer in our own way
And yes we're gonna have fun.

1. Classroom talk

2. Colours

| black | light blue | blue | dark blue | brown |

| light green | green | dark green | grey | orange |

| pink | purple | red | yellow | white |

hazel eyes

black hair

blond hair

red hair

3. Days of the week

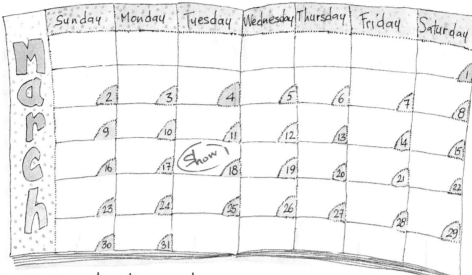

There are seven days in a week.
There are four weeks in a month.
There are twelve months in a year.

Did you know?
In English, the names of the days of the week always start with a capital letter. For example, *Today is **Monday**.*

4. Months of the year

AUGUST

NOVEMBER

SEPTEMBER

DECEMBER

OCTOBER

The four seasons

March, April, May = spring
June, July, August = summer
September, October, November = fall
December, January, February = winter

5. Time

3 o'clock

3:15 OR a quarter past three

3:30 OR half past three

3:45 OR a quarter to four

midnight

noon

morning = a.m.

afternoon = p.m.

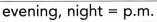

evening, night = p.m.

What time is it?

It's half past 10.

6. Numbers

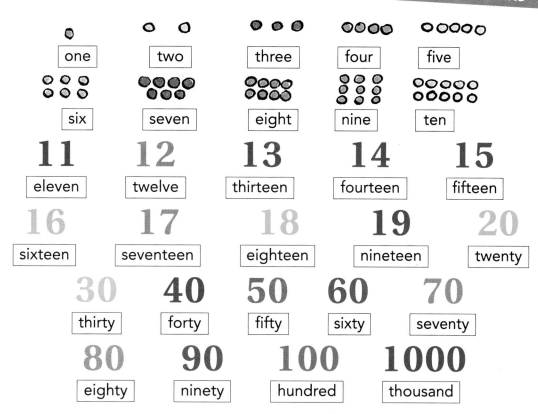

one — two — three — four — five

six — seven — eight — nine — ten

11 eleven	12 twelve	13 thirteen	14 fourteen	15 fifteen
16 sixteen	17 seventeen	18 eighteen	19 nineteen	20 twenty
30 thirty	40 forty	50 fifty	60 sixty	70 seventy
80 eighty	90 ninety	100 hundred	1000 thousand	

ORDINAL NUMBERS

ninth (9th)
eighth (8th)
seventh (7th)
tenth (10th)
sixth (6th)
fifth (5th)
fourth (4th)
third (3rd)
second (2nd)
first (1st)

187

7. Parts of the body

head

mouth

shoulder

arm

hand

wrist

elbow

finger

knee

leg

ankle

hair

foot

toe

eye

ear

cheek

nose

lips

8. Food

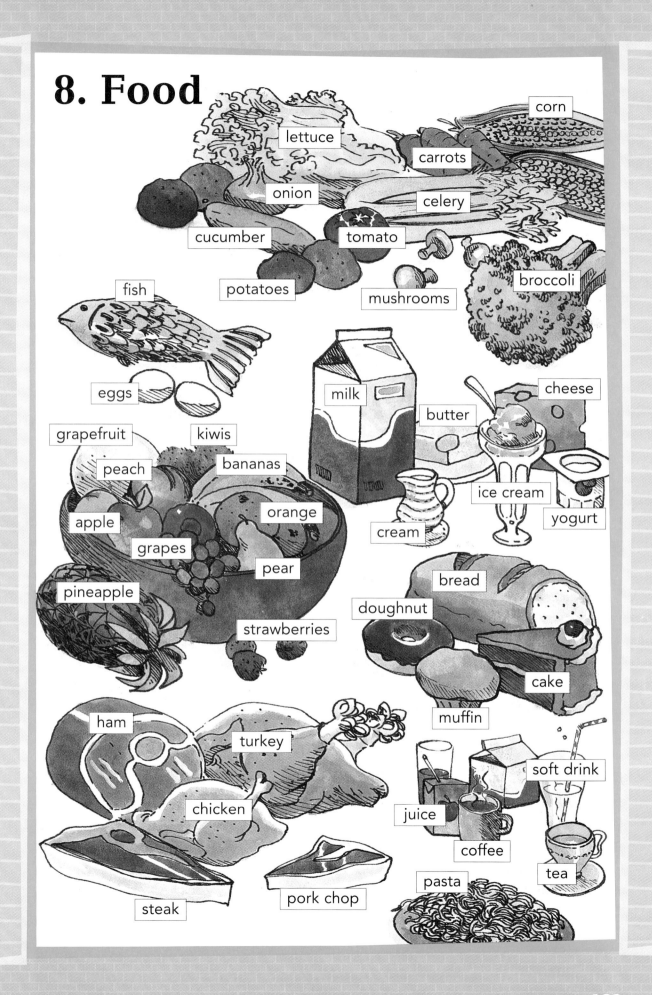

lettuce

corn

carrots

onion

celery

cucumber

tomato

broccoli

fish

potatoes

mushrooms

eggs

milk

butter

cheese

grapefruit

kiwis

peach

bananas

ice cream

yogurt

apple

orange

cream

grapes

pear

pineapple

bread

doughnut

strawberries

cake

muffin

ham

turkey

soft drink

chicken

juice

coffee

tea

pasta

steak

pork chop

9. Some useful expressions

Ways to greet people

Ways to say goodbye

Ways to say "That's dangerous"

Ways to congratulate someone

Ways to thank someone

Thank you.

Thanks.

Thanks a lot.

Thank you very much.

Ways to ask for help

Please can you help me?

Please give me a hand.

Ways to ask for clarification

Please say that again.

What does that mean?

Can you repeat that, please?

How do you say that in English?

I don't understand. Please can you explain?

Ways to apologize

Pardon me.

Sorry.

Sorry about that.

Excuse me.

I beg your pardon.

So sorry.

I'm very sorry.

10. Some useful question words

Questions about a thing (= What?)

Questions about a person (= Who?)

Questions about a place (= Where?)

Questions about time (= When? What time?)

Questions about feelings and age (= How?)

Questions about quantity (= How many? OR How much?)

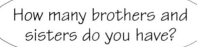

How many brothers and sisters do you have?

I have one half-sister and no brothers.

Just a small piece, please.

How much cake would you like?

Mom, I need a new bicycle helmet.

How much does it cost?

$19.95.

Questions about ability or permission (= Can?)

Can I go swimming with my friend, please?

Yes you can.

Can you swim under water?

Sure I can.